Continuous
Revival

Continuous
Revival

Norman Grubb

CLC ❖ PUBLICATIONS
Fort Washington, PA 19034

Published by CLC Publications

U.S.A.
P.O. Box 1449, Fort Washington, PA 19034

GREAT BRITAIN
51 The Dean, Alresford, Hants. SO24 9BJ

AUSTRALIA
P.O. Box 419M, Manunda, QLD 4879

NEW ZEALAND
10 MacArthur Street, Feilding

ISBN 0-87508-352-8

Contents

Preface

THESE few pages are an attempt to describe a revolutionary experience in my own life, and in that of many others, regarding the way of continuous revival. I am aware of no other truth from God which so simply and thoroughly reaches down to where ordinary folks live as does the secret of victorious living. By no means is this something which God has personally revealed to me alone. It is the working secret which has been bringing continuous revival to thousands in East Central Africa over a period of sixteen years.

The fact that there was such a thing as continuous revival first caught my interest some years ago when I heard of a constant movement of the Spirit in the area of the Ruanda Medical Mission (a field of the Church Missionary Society), for I felt that was exactly what we, in the ranks of our own mission, needed both at home and abroad. Various personal contacts with Africans and missionaries from the revival area deepened my conviction that God had given them the key we needed. In fact, I saw some of our own staff transformed and quickened into marvelous newness of life and ministry through quite short contacts with them. Finally the door of opportunity was opened to me in 1950 to pay a short visit myself to Ruanda and Uganda. As I had worked in Central Africa with C. T. Studd over a period of years, I had some understanding of African ways of life. What follows is an attempt to put into words what God taught me personally through that visit and what I have since found to be a blessing to many others.

First, there has been a new discovery by me and many others of what is meant by "revival." When we come down to it, in simplest form it means *the reviving of dead areas in our lives*. I remember when I first heard two men from Ruanda speaking very quietly and simply for two days in our London WEC headquarters to about ninety of our staff. At the last meeting, they very quietly opened the door for any present to say anything that was on their hearts. Very soon one and another were bringing to the light areas in their lives where they had come face to face with sin—unobserved by them before—and were bringing these transgressions to the cleansing blood. I got a real shock at the end when one of the two quietly said, "I don't know if you realize it, friends, but this is revival!"

The transforming truth of that statement took time to sink in—and is still sinking in! It began to shake me out of the misconception of years—that revival could come only in great soul-shaking outpourings of the Spirit. Thank God for such torrents when they do come; they have been the great and precious hurricanes of the Spirit in the history of the Church. But I saw the defeatism and almost hopelessness that so many of us had fallen into by thinking that we could do nothing about revival except pray (often rather unbelievingly) and wait until the heavens opened and God came down. But now I see that "revival" in its truest sense is an everyday affair right down within the reach of everyday folk—to be experienced each day in our hearts, homes, churches and fields of service.

When revival does burst forth in greater and more public ways, thank God! But meanwhile we should see to it that we are being ourselves constantly revived persons . . . which, of course, also means that others are getting revived in our own circles. By this means God can have channels of revival by the thousands in all the churches of the world! And this is just what I found in Africa, and what I am attempting to describe in these pages; not, all glory and praise to God, just the passing on of a mere theory, but what has come to me by living with and seeing continuous revival in action among communities of hundreds in Africa; by experiencing the same working of the Spirit in my own life; by examining and grasping in some measure the Scriptural basis of this continuous revival; and finally, by seeing God move in revival in many others through the presentation of the message and testimony. It has been a matter of seeing, learning, experiencing and transmitting, and now endeavoring to outline the reality in print.

The truth is that revival is really *the Reviver in action*, and He came two thousand years ago at Pentecost. Revival is not so much a vertical out-pouring from heaven (for the Reviver is *already* here in His temple, the bodies of the redeemed) as it is a horizontal outmoving of the Reviver through these temples into the world. It is a *horizontal* rather than a *vertical* movement, and the importance of this fact will be seen later.

Norman P. Grubb
1952

1

The Walk

NOW to go into the matter point by point. I learned first a wholly new emphasis on the WALK of the Christian. I learned that in our evangelical and rightful zeal to bring sinners to the crisis of the new birth, and to lead the saints on to further crises of separation, consecration, sanctification, the baptism of the Holy Spirit, or whatever might be the special emphasis of our various Christian communities, we have often made too much of the spiritual *crises* and too little of the *walk*.

But the Scriptures leave us in no doubt of their emphasis. In almost every epistle the Holy Spirit leads us on *through* the crises—the way into Christ—to the WALK with Him. Thus in Romans we are taught the way of justification and sanctification from chapter 1 through 7; then in 8 it says, "There is therefore now no condemnation to them which are in Christ Jesus, who *walk* not after the flesh, but after the Spirit." In

Galatians there is the battle of justification by faith as against works; and then Paul says, "This I say then, *Walk* in the Spirit, and ye shall not fulfill the lusts of the flesh." And later, "If we live [have come alive] in the Spirit, let us also *walk* in the Spirit." In Ephesians he introduces us into our glorious union with the ascended Christ, and then says, "I therefore, the prisoner of the Lord, beseech you that ye *walk* worthy of the vocation wherewith ye are called"; and later, "*Walk* not as other Gentiles walk . . . *walk* in love . . . *walk* as children of light . . . *walk* circumspectly."

In Colossians he says, "As ye have therefore received Christ Jesus the Lord, so *walk* in Him." In I Thessalonians he rejoices in the saving power of the gospel in the lives of the young converts, and then says, "As ye have received of us how ye ought to *walk* and to please God, so ye would abound more and more."

Finally, to mention only one more passage, John in his first epistle takes us to the very heights when he says we are to "*walk* as He walked," for "as He is, so are we in the world." Indeed, John here does not even discuss how to be born again or how to abide in Christ, but, taking these for granted, now talks about the walk and life which is the outcome. (See also verses in II John and

III John.)

Now to walk is a step-by-step activity. Given the main destination, all that matters is the next step. Christian living is concerned, therefore, just with the implications of the *present* moment, not with past or future. But we tend to live in the past and thus to avoid the keen edge of the challenge of the immediate moment. Thus, as things arise in our hearts and lives which are not consistent with our Christian testimony, we say, or imply, "Well, I know these things are not right, but anyhow I have been born again, I have been cleansed in His blood, I have received eternal life; Christ lives in me." Thus I circle around the raw facts of my immediate condition by leaning back in dependence on my past crises. We make too much of past happenings but too little of the present walk. Thank God we are born again and have received other impartations of grace, but now let us forget those, as it were. Let us remember that all we are asked to do is to "WALK WITH JESUS," and that means simple concentration on things as they are with me just this moment . . . then the next . . . then the next . . . and so on.

There is something else also that much affects our Christian experience when we get confused between looking back to crises and just living moment by moment. One of Satan's favorite weapons is false condemnation. He loves to make us look back at our past failures, or into the future at our probably equal failures (so he says), and then put us into a tailspin of despair or depression. "Look at your pride, coldness, sensuality, worldliness, fruitlessness. You say you were born again or sanctified. Look at yourself! And if you have been that in the past, believe me, you will be exactly the same in the future!" In other words, Satan likes to talk in long-term generalities, based indeed on an element of truth, but built up into a huge lie; for God does not look on His children in a general sense as proud, cold, fruitless, and so on. He sees them in Christ, being conformed to the image of His Son. The difference between Satan's condemnations and God's convictions is that where Satan uses generalities pointing back to the past or forward to the future, God sees past and future in Christ and just deals with the present, and deals specifically. We *walk* moment by moment, step by step with Him, the past under the blood, the future in His keeping. We are in Jesus and He in us. Now then, if our walk at this moment is darkened with clouds because of the rising up of some motion of sin in us, then God just points to that. "There," He says, "look at that, *just* that.

Just get that quickly under the blood and then walk again with Me." So simple, so free from these condemnations from the past (or excuses through leaning back on the past crises) and from those fears for the future.

So now we have the *first point* in continuous revival. We "walk with Jesus." We are concerned only with the step-by-step life. We live in the present: "Today, today, today," as it says five times in Hebrews 3 through 4. We do not excuse the present by leaning back on past spiritual crises, nor do we get under false condemnation or fear through looking back at the past or forward into the future.

2

Brokenness

THE next point is BROKENNESS. "Broken" is a picturesque word, a key word, indeed *the* key word, in continuous revival. It is not a word that is found a great deal in Scripture (though more often than we think, should we examine a concordance), but it occurs frequently enough to show that it is a picturesque as well as true way of describing the sinner's only and constant relationship to his Savior.

We first learn that salvation is only possible for lost men through a *broken* Savior: "This is my body which is *broken* for you"; "Reproach hath *broken* my heart." In Gethsemane Christ had a broken will, and on Calvary a broken fellowship even with His Father; for the One who is our Substitute and who was made sin for us had to take upon Himself the proud, unbroken ego of fallen man, and had to be broken at Calvary in his place. But man also has to be "broken." He sees his sinful condition before God as he realizes the coming judgment and wrath, and as he is pointed to the slain Lamb he has to "break" at the foot of the cross. The proud, self-justifying, self-reliant, self-seeking self has to come simply as a lost, undone sinner, whose only hope is a justifying Savior. David said it well when, at the supreme moment of his own total brokenness, in Psalm 51, the Spirit caused him to comment, "The sacrifices of God are a *broken* spirit; a *broken* and a contrite heart, O God, Thou wilt not despise."

Here we come to a crucial point concerning the way of brokenness, as indeed concerning all relationships of the Christian life. It is the most crucial point in this whole way of continuous revival—the point, as we shall see later, that needs to be relearned by twentieth-century Christians surrounded by all their respectability. It is this. All Christian relationships are *two-way*, not *one-way*. They are *horizontal* as well as *vertical*. That is to say, we are a two-way people. We are not just isolated units living in a vertical relationship with an isolated God; we are members of a human family also, with whom we live in horizontal relationships, and our obligations are two-way all the time.

We cannot, for instance, say that we have become righteous before God through faith in

Christ and yet continue unrighteous among men. The Bible says that would be living a lie. Equally, we cannot say we love God and yet hate our brother, for the Bible says, "He that loveth not his brother whom he hath seen, how can he love God whom he hath not seen?" This comes across particularly in John's first epistle, where the two-way fellowship is mentioned in the first chapter at verse three, two-way righteousness in the third chapter at verse seven, and two-way love in the fourth chapter at verse twenty.

Even more does this apply to the way of brokenness, that is, with regard to repentance and faith. "The word of faith," we read in Romans 10:8–10, is two-way, with the heart towards God and with the mouth before man. Indeed, Paul takes it further and says that to experience in our hearts and lives the full benefit of our faith, we must express it *both* ways, for "with the heart man believes unto righteousness" (that is to say, the heart-believer is accounted righteous before God) but it is "with the mouth" that "confession is made unto salvation" (that is to say, we thus realize in our experience the joyful fact that we are saved).

Confession before man does something in our hearts that heart-faith alone can never do. There are many sincere believers who attend churches where they are not taught to witness before men or to expect assurance of salvation. These people truly trust in the mercies of God through Christ, yet do not really know for sure in their hearts that they are saved; and they have none of the joy of the Lord because there is no *mouth confession*. But when such believers do the much-more-costly thing of telling men that Christ has become their Savior, something happens in their hearts. They are saved and *know* they are saved!

Any soul-winner with spiritual insight understands that if a seeker were to say, "Yes, I'll accept Christ now, but I don't think I'll let anybody know," he would respond, "Brother, that's not genuine faith or brokenness. If you really mean business and are really committed as a lost sinner to the mercies of your Savior, the proof is that you are committed before men as well as God. If you don't confess before men, we Christians may rightly doubt the genuineness of your faith and the reality of your salvation."

So saving faith—the attitude of brokenness— is a two-way activity, towards God and man, as are righteousness and love and indeed all the relationships of Christian living. Let me put it this way. We can liken a man to a house. It has a roof and walls. So also man in his fallen state has a roof on top of his sins, coming between him and God; and he also has walls up, between him and his neighbor. But at salvation, when broken at the cross, not only does the roof come off through faith in Christ but the walls fall down flat, and the man's true condition as a sinner-saved-by-grace is confessed before all men.

Unfortunately, the trouble soon begins again after conversion—and here lies the basic hindrance to continued revival. Continued revival is continued brokenness; but brokenness is two-way, and that means walls kept down as well as roof off. But man's most deep-rooted and subtle sin is the subtle sin of *pride*: self-esteem and self-respect. Though hardly realizing it, while we are careful to keep the roof off between ourselves and God through repentance and faith, we soon let those walls of respectability creep up again between ourselves and our brethren. We don't mind our brethren knowing about the successes we have in our Christian living. If we win a soul, if we lead a class, if we have a prayer answered, if we get good ideas from the Scriptures—we don't mind if they hear about these things, because we get a little reflected credit because of them. But where we fail, in those many, many areas of our daily lives—that is a different question! If God has to deal with us over our impatience or temper in the home, over dishonesty in our business, over coldness or some other sin, by no means do we easily bear testimony to our brethren of God's faithful and gracious dealings in such areas of failure. Why not? Just because of pride, self-esteem, although we would often more conveniently call it reserve! The fact is, we love the praise of men as well as of God, and that is exactly what the Scriptures say stops the flow of confession before men (John 12:42–43).

But let us note that the key to the reality of the whole of the Scriptures is the openness of the men of the Bible. We know of God's most intimate dealings with them, their sins and failures every bit as much as their successes. How do we have knowledge of the details of Abraham's false step with Hagar, of Jacob's tricks with Isaac and Esau, of Moses' private act of disobedience concerning speaking to the rock? Of Elijah's flight and God's secret rebuke, of the inner history of Jonah? How did the disciples acquire the inside story of Jesus' temptations to record them for us? Only because they were all open before their contemporaries. They lived in the light with each other as with God.

All through history, when buffeted by fears and sorrows and doubts, men have turned to the psalms. Why? Because these detail the heart experiences of men in fear and doubt and guilt and soul-hunger, describing how they have felt and how God has met them.

Why was David's repentance acceptable to God, and yet Saul's—for a much less apparently carnal sin of failing to slaughter all the Amalekites—unacceptable? The reason is plain. Both kings, when faced respectively by the accusing finger of the prophets Nathan and Samuel, admitted their guilt before God and said, "I have sinned" (I Samuel 15:24 and II Samuel 12:13); but Saul's repentance was demonstrated to be insincere because he desired that his sin be hidden from the people (I Samuel 15:30), whereas the proof of David's utter brokenness was that he told the whole world in Psalm 51 what a sinner he was and that his only hope was in God's mercy. Openness before man is the genuine proof of sincerity before God, even as righteousness before man and love to man are the genuine proofs of righteousness before God and love to God.

Note also that hiding the truth about ourselves before men—pretending to be better than we really are—is the supreme sin which Jesus drove home to the Pharisees, the sin of hypocrisy, and was the direct cause of their crucifying Him. It was not the open harlot or publican but the religious men who pretended to be holy and covered their inner condition who drove Jesus to the cross. They did this rather than have the truth about themselves exposed any more. Note also that the first sin judged in the early church was the sin of hiddenness before men: Ananias and Sapphira pretending before their brethren that they were making a bigger surrender than they really were.

Finally, note that in every dealing of the believer with God recorded in the Bible—every step taken in the walk of faith—Scripture shows that that transaction of inner faith had to be expressed in the spoken word: the faith had to be *confessed* before men. It was the clinching act which sealed the faith and committed the believers. See it in the lives of all men of faith— from Abraham right through to the apostles. What they had believed in their heart, they declared with the mouth as something God had said to them and which would assuredly come to pass.

So far, then, we have learned *these two lessons*: that continuous revival is a simple daily walking with Jesus, and that it means walking in a two-way brokenness which is expressed in the heart to God and by the mouth before men. We will see in a moment, in practical detail, how this works out more fully in our daily life.

3

Cups Running Over

WE will now turn to the first chapter of John's first epistle to lead us further in this "walking." Verse 3 speaks at the beginning of a two-way fellowship: ". . . that ye also may have fellowship with us," and "truly our fellowship is with the Father and with His Son, Jesus Christ." Then it goes on in verse 4 to say that he writes to us "that your joy may be full." Fullness of joy is to characterize this daily walk. Or as David said in Psalm 23, "My cup runneth over," not only full, but running over! And this brings us to our third major point. Walking with Jesus, brokenness, and now CUPS RUNNING OVER.

We all can recognize those words as a beautiful description of the abiding presence of Jesus in the heart, His peace, joy and presence filling us to overflowing, with no shadow between. We can visualize the clear, sparkling water of life welling up within and flowing over the thirsty souls around us through look and word and deed.

But here comes the point of it in this message of revival. We are to recognize that "cups running over" is the *normal* daily experience of the believer walking with Jesus—not the abnormal or occasional, but the normal, continuous experience.

But that just isn't so in the lives of practically all of us. Those cups running over get pretty muddled up; other things besides the joy of the Lord flow out of us. We are often much more conscious of emptiness, or dryness, or hardness, or disturbance, or fear, or worry than we are of the fullness of His presence and overflowing joy and peace. And now comes the point. What stops that moment-by-moment flow? The answer is only one thing—sin. But we by no means usually accept or recognize that. We have many other more convenient names for those disturbances of heart. We say it is nerves that causes us to speak impatiently—not sin. We say it is tiredness that causes us to speak the sharp word at home—not sin. We say it is the pressure of work which causes us to lose our peace, get worried, act or speak hastily—not sin. We say it is our difficult or hurtful neighbor who causes us resentment or dislike, or even hate—but not sin. Anything but sin. We go to psychiatrists or psychologists to get inner problems unraveled—tension, strain, disquiet, dispeace—but anything which causes the cups to cease running over is SIN.

What proof have we of that statement? Quite a simple one. What are "cups running over"? Of course, the Spirit witnessing to Jesus in the heart. He is our peace, joy, life, all, and it is the Spirit's work never to cease witnessing to Him within us. What then can stop the Spirit's witness? Can nerves, or tiredness, or pressure of circumstances, or difficult people? Paul's cry was, "Who or what can separate me from the love of God? Can tribulation or persecution or things present or things to come? No!" he says. Only one thing separates us from Him—"your iniquities have separated between you and your God, and your sins have hid His face from you." Thank God, the great separation has been replaced by reunion with Him at Calvary . . . but still the daily incursions of sin in the heart bring about the temporary separation from the sense of His presence; we all know that. The cups do not run over.

Now this is an exceedingly important point. By far the largest number of us, including me, have not been accustomed to regard it as some form of sin if the cups cease to run over, and that is just why they do not quickly start running over again. For where sin is seen to be sin and confessed as such, the blood is also seen to be the blood, praise God, ever cleansing from all unrighteousness; and where the blood cleanses, the Spirit always witnesses—and the cups run over again. But the blood never cleanses *excuses*—sin called by some more polite name!

4

Conviction, Confession, Cleansing

HERE then are the three main points of the walk in continuous revival—Walking with Jesus, Brokenness, Cups Running Over. But when cups do not run over, which is very often—then what?

Only sin stops the inner witness. Then how are we to know what the sin is? The answer to that is to be found by reading on in this key chapter of I John 1. Verse 3 has spoken of two-way fellowship, and verse 4 of fullness of joy. Verse 5 gives a surprise. John says he is now going to give us the inner truth about Him with whom we walk. He is . . . love? No—"God is light." If it just said "love," that would be easy, for I might escape a too strict facing of sin by saying, "Well, anyhow He loves"—which is indeed what I have often said. But "this is the message . . . God is light."

What does that mean? Well, nothing could be more simple. The obvious main function of light is to reveal things as they are. The Scriptures themselves state: "Whatever maketh manifest is light . . ." (Ephesians 5:13). Light is very silent, does not push or drive anyone away, but is inescapable to any honest person. You can't lie to light. If you hit your toe against an object in the dark, you may mistakenly say that it is a table. But when the light is turned on in the room, you can no longer continue to say that it is a table if it really is a piano. Light just gives you the lie.

God is light. Silently, inexorably He shines on and in us, revealing things just as they are in His sight. Have you ever noticed the pivotal place given, even in salvation, to our response to light? In John 3, we are distinctly told that men are not lost because of their sins (for they have already been atoned for) but they are lost for refusing the light. "This is the condemnation, that light is come into the world, but men loved darkness rather than light, because their deeds were evil." Light silently showed them exactly what they are in God's holy sight, but they won't acknowledge it. No, they will never "come to the light" and admit themselves to be what God says they are. But the only way any of us have been saved has been by responding to that light and saying about ourselves what God says. Thus our eternal destiny hangs on whether we love darkness or come to the light.

But even as this is true concerning the unsaved and the necessity of their "coming to the light," it is also true in I John 1 of the believer and the necessity of his "walking in the light." He also can walk in darkness (verse 6) if he wishes to do so. That is to say, he can refuse to admit, concerning himself, what God says about him; he can have other and more convenient names for his sins. Worse still, he can be either a deliberate hypocrite (saying he has fellowship with Him, but really walking in the darkness), or he can be self-deceived and not recognize that he is sinning when he is saying he has no sin (verse 8).

So it gets down to this. Sin is a revelation. It is God who graciously shows us sin, even as it is He who shows us the precious blood. Sin is only seen to be SIN—against God—when He reveals it; otherwise sin may just be known as a wrong against a brother, or an antisocial act, or an inconvenience, or a disability, or some such thing. Indeed that is often the extent of the message of a "social gospel"—to be rid of sin as a hindrance to brotherhood, as an inconvenience to human progress; not as coming short of the glory of God. GOD shows us sin. We do not need to keep looking inside ourselves. This is not a life of introspection or morbid self-examination. We do not walk with sin, we walk with Jesus; but, as we walk in childlike faith and fellowship with Him step by step, moment by moment, then if the cups cease to run over, He who is light, with whom we are walking, will clearly show us what the sin *is* which is hindering—what its real name is in His sight, rather than the pseudonym, the excusing title, which we might find it more convenient to call it.

Let us say again, it is so simple. God does not speak in terms of general condemnation, leading to despair of the past or to fear of the future. He speaks in simple, specific terms of any actual sin in the present which is hindering the inner witness of His Spirit.

What do we do then? Well, that is obvious. I John 1:9 says, "If we confess our sins. . . ." The word *confess* is the word *say* with the preposition *con* meaning *with* added. Three times over in those verses 5–10 man has said his own say (verses 6, 8, 10); but to confess is to say with another, to say what another says. To confess is to say about my sin what God says about it. "You say that is sin, Lord; so do I." That is confession;

of course, companied by the desire to be rid of the sin, and an actual ceasing to do the thing or maintain the attitude, whatever it may be.

Then where there is this confession, we all know there is the word of promise: "If we confess our sins, He is faithful and just to forgive us our sins, and to cleanse us from all unrighteousness." We may say the cleansing is almost automatic, where there is the confession. That light which shines so unchangingly on the sin shines also on the blood. "If we walk in the light, as He is in the light," says John, "we have fellowship one with another, and the blood of Jesus Christ His Son cleanseth us from all sin." When walking in the light, we read, both sin and the precious blood are seen—the one, praise God, canceling out the other. And it is important to remember that confession of sin does not deliver by itself. It is *the blood* that cleanses, and we must always pass on from confession to faith and praise for *the blood*, believing that the blood alone is what glorifies God and delivers us. Folk often remain depressed and mournful and asking others to pray for them after confession of sin, when they ought to pass straight on by simple faith to the blood ever flowing and cleansing, as in the words of the old hymn:

> *The cleansing blood, I see, I see;*
> *I plunge, and oh, it cleanses me.*
> *It cleanses me, it cleanses me;*
> *Oh praise the Lord, it cleanses me.*

Once again, where the blood cleanses, the Spirit witnesses, and where the Spirit witnesses, the cups always run over! So we are back again where we started—walking with Jesus step by step, brokenness, cups running over. When they stop running over, it is always sin. Sin is seen as sin in the light of God. As we walk in that light, we recognize and confess our sins; the blood cleanses; the Spirit witnesses; and the cups run over again!

5

Testimony

BUT that is not all. That is still leaving out the further step which is the missing link in our evangelical living—the very link which releases the revival in our hearts and others. Remember again that saving faith, the first act of brokenness, was a two-way faith. Remember that the costly part of that faith was not the heart-believing before God but the mouth-confession before men. Remember that, while it cost more, it gave us more; for as we confessed before men, it was as if Jesus confessed us before God His Father in heaven, and the Spirit confessed the Savior in our hearts. The joy of the Lord became our strength; we were saved. Finally, remember that the mouth-committal horizontally was the real proof of the genuineness of the heart-committal before God.

Initial brokenness was roof off, walls down. But now in the daily life? Roof still off, but what about the walls? Continued brokenness is continued revival, and continued brokenness has implicit in it the continued two-way testimony. But here we want to watch carefully. The confession that matters in the Scripture, and which is most referred to, is the confession of CHRIST, rather than of sin (although there are such verses as I John 1:9 and James 5:16—where "faults" is, in the original, "sins") and it is to the constant confession of Christ that I am called. That is my duty. That is my privilege. That is the way both to get blessing and to transmit it. Indeed, perhaps the word *confession* has become so misused through its use in the confessional that it is better and clearer to use the word *testimony*. Testimony to Christ is our duty and privilege. Now the first testimony we made had no reserves about it. We were sinners and said so. Probably in many cases our sins were already known in our community, and the liquor addict, the gambler, the loose-liver, the proud, the self-righteous, the dishonest one, gives open glory to God that he has been saved from these things through the power of the precious blood. The emphasis is not on the sin, although that may be mentioned, but on the Savior from sin. It is not a morbid self-revelation but a glorious magnification of Christ.

Now it is that form of daily testimony which is the missing note in our present-day Christianity. We were sinners and were saved. We gloried in saying so. But we still so often "come short of the glory of God" in daily life. No longer those old, deliberate, gross sins of the fallen days, or old false attitudes of pure self-centeredness or pride; for if we are that, we are not saved. But we know too well we are still open to the assaults of Satan. The flesh still makes its appeal to us, and we respond, although our normal position in Christ is "not in the flesh, but in the Spirit" (Romans 8:9). Even those who have entered into a sanctified experience by faith, and the witness of the Spirit, as in my own case, making real in their experience such statements as in Acts 15:8–9, Galatians 2:20, Ephesians 2:6, still know constant temptation. The cases must indeed be rare where Satan does not make actual inroads by some subtle form of sin, either by unbelief, fear, worry, depression, hardness towards a brother, dislike, self-pity, pride, coldness of heart, impatience, criticism, unkind thoughts, the sharp word, jealousy, envy, partiality, hypocrisy, strife, the lust of the eye, evil or impure thoughts, sloth, selfishness, and the like.

So now, as we entered the way of salvation by a two-way brokenness, we must continue in the way in the daily walk. Something comes in which stops the flow of the Spirit. It is seen to be sin,

however "small" we may like to call it (Is any
sin small which crucified my Lord?); it is confessed and forgiven. But brokenness is two-way.
There is the testimony to give before men, as
God gives the opening. Nothing need stop me
giving it except that it would hurt my pride, my
self-esteem. That is how I glorify God—by testifying, as occasion arises, to His fresh deliverances, the fresh experiences of the power of His
cleansing blood in my life. Some would narrow
this down and say, "Should we not merely put a
sin right with any against whom we might have
committed it, such as hard words between husband and wife, and leave it at that?" Certainly
the sin must be put right with those against whom
it was committed, but the testimony to God's
deliverance belongs to the whole Church. For
actually no sin is committed privately. None of
us lives unto himself. Our faces, our attitudes,
our very atmosphere is poisoning or blessing all
those with whom we come in contact. A quarrel
between husband and wife, for instance, reaches
out in its effect far beyond those two. It affects
the whole household. It affects visitors in the
home, workmates in the business, and above all
fellow-believers in the church. Remember, it is
not a question of confessing sin but of praising
for a deliverance, and giving others the chance

of praising with us.

Daily testimony before men in this way is an ever-fresh confession of a saving Christ; but to be honest testimony, it involves some account of what the deliverance is from. It is that which puts teeth into the testimony. It is also proof of our genuine repentance and genuine brokenness, just as confession before men at conversion was the proof of the reality of my new-found faith. To be really wide open before God and man is to be ready at all times to tell of His dealings with me.

It is yet more than that—and this is of utmost importance. We remember that it was the confession of Christ before men that made Him so real to our own hearts. It did something for us which mere heart-faith did not. Now it is just the same concerning the daily walk. The real reason why we are usually so insensitive to the "little" sins of our daily walk, and why we pass them over without much concern, is just because we are not too ashamed about them, or not too repentant, or even in some cases we have given up hope of any lasting deliverance. And why so? Because, while we walk with only the roof off and deal in secret with God alone about our daily affairs, we have the convenient sense of a God of great mercy, of a Christ who died for

us, of our security in Him, of an easy-going for-
giveness—and so, frankly, we do not get too
concerned about our present inconsistencies! But
if we start walking in the light with others about
the Lord's daily dealings with us, telling them
when the shadow of sin has darkened our path
and how God has dealt with us over it, we shall
suddenly find two things: one, that we have an
altogether new sense of shame for sin; and two,
an altogether new sense of cleansing and liberation from the sin.

We just have to face the fact that we are very
human, and our human relationships are usually
more vivid to us than our fellowship with God.
Thus we have a far more vivid sense of shame
about a sin when we tell our brethren than when
we just tell God. It is a simple fact that this
openness before men does something in us. It
sharpens us up concerning daily sin as never before. It is part of the secret of daily revival. It is
amazing how, when walking in the light with
our brethren as well as with God, we begin to
come alive to attitudes, or actions, of sin in our
lives which we just never noticed to be sin before, or perhaps we took for granted would always be part of our makeup.

With all this there is also the effect on others
of this open testifying. We know that the way

salvation is spread is by our telling the unsaved
what the Lord has done for us; it does something
in their hearts, quickening a desire for the same
experience. So it is with testimony among God's
people. The joy and praise leaps from one heart
to another when we hear what the Lord has done
for another. The more direct, open, and exact
the testimony, the more we rejoice. It does yet
more. It convicts. Our hearts are fashioned alike.
The way the devil tempts you is almost certainly
the way he tempts me. When I hear you tell of
the Lord's dealings down where you really live
in your home relationships, in your business, and
so on, it surely reaches me on some spot where I
need the same light and deliverance. That is
exactly how great revivals break out and spread.
The way is always the same. Sin is suddenly seen
to be sin in some life. Someone breaks down
(brokenness) and doesn't mind who is present;
he can only see himself as a sinner needing re-
newed cleansing. So out he comes, maybe with
tears; public reconciliations are made; the conviction spreads, till dozens are doing the same
thing. "Revival has visited this church," we say
with joy. So don't you see that when there is a
continuous sensitiveness to the smallest sin that
stops the cups running over, when there is rec-
ognition of the sin in the light, confession, for-

giveness, and the thankful public testimony to
the glory of God of what the Lord has done,
there is a daily revival?

Yet one more point on this heart of the matter. Many of God's people, including the writer,
know something of God's deliverances from sin;
but there is some spot still in the life which may
be given the name mentioned in Hebrews 12:1,
"the sin which doth so easily beset us"; and at
this "weak spot" we really give up any idea that
God can really, fully, and permanently deliver.
It may not be some big thing, as the world calls
big; perhaps it is so hidden that it is just a mere
touch of sin known only to the person himself
("the garment spotted by the flesh") but hope of
full deliverance is really given up. Then we en-
ter into this revival walk in the light step by
step. We are made sensitive as never before both
to the reality and the shamefulness of sin. We
find that as we walk brokenly with God and one
another, sins which used to beset us easily lessen
in their power and falls are fewer. Then it suddenly comes to us as new light that this special
spot of weakness, taken for granted through the
years, can be dealt with and deliverance found,
if recognized as sin to be faced and hated each
time it arises—the emphasis not being so much
on a once-for-all crisis deliverance but on the

daily and immediate dealing with the evil thing the moment it shows itself. Another discovery may be that the reason why our besetting sin does not get dealt with is that we find a certain sweetness in the flesh—not in actual sin, of course, but on the outer edges of it, as it were. That sweetness has to be recognized as a manifestation of the flesh, and must be hated. Indeed, true repentance is hatred, and where there *is* hatred of sin—God's hatred in us (Hebrews 1:9)—power for deliverance is found in the blood.

In this walking with one another in the light, careful distinction must also be made between temptation and sin. Many earnest souls continue in bondage and under false accusation because they are looking for the impossible—deliverance from even temptation; and also because they mistake temptation for sin, and accept condemnation and a sense of defilement when they should not do so. It also makes them confused about how far to go in open testimony and fellowship.

Temptation is continuous and will be while we are in this fallen world. Jesus as man was tempted in all points like as we are, and frequently—"Ye are they that have continued with me in my temptations." There is a difference between temptation and sin—James 1:14–15 makes this plain. Temptation is the stimulation of our natural desires (the correct meaning of "lust" in verse 14), whether physical appetites or the faculties of soul or spirit. Jesus was tempted in all these three realms on the Mount of Temptation. But the sudden impulse to think this wrong thought, or to say this or do that, the attraction of the eye in an unlawful direction, the first motion of fear, worry, resentment, and so on, is temptation for which we are not held responsible as willful sin. It is "when lust [desire] hath conceived, it bringeth forth sin." It is when we allow the temptation to find lodgement in us, when we continue the wrong thought, allow the resentment to remain, keep on looking, speak the hasty word, and so on, that temptation has become sin. Obviously, therefore, if we withstand the temptation as it arises, by abiding in Christ, we should not accept condemnation, and our testimony to His praise should be to His keeping power in the evil day.

Let us also be watchful to maintain liberty in the matter of testimony. How easily we can slip back to legalism instead of walking in the glorious liberty of the sons of God. We can endeavor to walk by rule instead of by the gentle but free compulsions of the Spirit who leads, not drives. Thus we can get into the bondage of thinking that we are under strict compulsion to testify to the Lord's dealings on all or on fixed occasions. Testimony of this kind can become as much a set form with one group as absence of any testimony is a set form with another! We must never allow ourselves to be driven. We are not mere human imitators, feeling compelled to say something just because our brother does, or because it is the usual thing on certain occasions. We "walk with Jesus" even in the matter of testimony. There should be a divine compulsion—when we know from Him within by inner conviction that we must open our lips, and when we can draw power from Him to do so; that is quite a different thing from the drive of the law, or of imitation. Sometimes the best testimony might be to testify that God has given me nothing to say! "Stand fast, therefore, in the liberty wherewith Christ hath made us free, and be not entangled again in the yoke of bondage."

Equally we must avoid that subtle pressure on others to see the same as ourselves, and that subtle criticism of those who do not. Of course we want others to have any light God has given us; but it was God who *gave* it us in His own time and way. Let us, then, leave it to God to *give* it to our brethren as He pleases. Our only job is humbly and joyfully to testify to what God shows *us*. It is impressive in the Gospel of John to note the calm Jesus manifested among His fierce critics and opponents—on the simple basis that people can only see and receive what God *gives* them to see.

Thus, this living in revival, personally and in our community, is the freedom of the Spirit. It is not a question of forming new sects or fellowships or cliques which cause divisions in churches and give an "I am holier than thou" impression. It is just to live in revival, in the light, in brokenness, in cleansing, in testimony, just as God leads—in the home, in the church, everywhere.

Questions are sometimes asked about to whom we should testify and if there should be any reservations in our testimony. Should we, for instance, tell unsaved people of the Lord's personal dealings with us? Perhaps a simple answer, subject always to the individual guidance of the Spirit, would be that we should always testify even to the most opposed and indifferent if we have sinned in a way which was obvious to them, such as by heated words. It is to the glory of God that we humble ourselves before them and tell them of the Lord's gracious restoration, as we have repented. But if our testimony is concerning things in our lives about which the Lord has dealt with us unknown to our unsaved friends, then it may be that we should keep that testimony for our brethren in Christ.

As for reservations in testimony, one matter about which wisdom and restraint may be needed is those sins which have such a deep hold on all mankind and which take first place in all lists of sins in the Scriptures—uncleanness, debauchery, impure thoughts, fornication, adultery. God has put a barrier between the sexes which it is His will we preserve, and therefore in mixed meetings only veiled language can be used in referring to these things. Yet at the same time, of all temptations and sins this is the one which in one form or another eats most deeply into lives. Maybe the only way in which we can go to the bottom in the light with God and one another in this respect is when men get together among themselves, and women likewise. And there certainly is a need for this.

Perhaps no criticism is more strongly made against open fellowship than when someone speaks in the open unadvisedly on sex matters. It seems as if the human mind leaps to seize on this. We have all heard stories of such indiscretions, and sometimes they are used to discredit open fellowship. Certainly, as we have said, they should be avoided and discouraged, and I found that the maturing fellowships in Africa, where

one might expect more "raw" testimonies from
new believers coming up from the grossness of
heathendom, have learned to stop any such statements and to tell the speaker just to say that
God had been dealing with him over the sins of
impurity. But I would also say this. Why do we
express such disgust when an unwisely open testimony is given? Here is some poor soul deep in
the mire of these loathsome sins but at last coming to the light, finding the glorious power of
the blood and not recognizing, perhaps through
the past defilement of his mind, that such things
should not be talked about; in his zeal and new-
found joy, or perhaps under deep conviction,
he pours out the sewerage of his soul. Is God
shocked? I reckon not. I reckon that the joy in
heaven over a poor soul delivered and cleansed
is more than any distress at his unwise statements. Look how open the Bible is! So let us
keep a balance in these things. Let us avoid saying things which could put unclean thoughts into
the minds of others, or which are not seemly;
but if such things are said in honesty but with
unwise zeal, let us not be over alarmed but look
for an occasion for a quiet word in season concerning restraint on future occasions.

Brokenness is obedience; indeed, revival is the
simple outcome of obedience to the light. But

for many of us the brokenness to which we are now referring, including openness before men, starts by being really *costly*. The reason is obvious. The walls of reserve and self-esteem have gone very high, probably without our ever realizing it, and so the first step into this brokenness is probably a big one. It is the walls of Jericho which have to fall down flat! I certainly found that, and so have many others. In my own case I suddenly found myself face to face in Central Africa with a brother whom I had met and disliked in England! I had disliked him only because he was too open for my taste, although I had not at that time traced the real cause of my dislike; I was not ready enough for the light in those days. But here I was in a revival company where dislike was only another word for *hate*—which was faced and brought to the light as sin; and I was carefully pretending that I had brotherly love for a man whom in the white-and-black terms of I John, I "hated"! It was then I found how high those walls of pride are. I just could not bring myself to admit in public that I had the sin of dislike against him, and equally the sin of hypocrisy against all my brethren in pretending that I did like him. As a senior visiting missionary, I could not let on that I had such a "foolish" thing in my heart. But it was not foolish—it was sin which crucified my Lord. To say I could not bring it out was to deceive myself; I could, but I wouldn't, that was all. I had to learn obedience to the light. At last, after two days under the constant inner compulsion of the Spirit, I just took the step of cold-blooded obedience, brought it into the light before the brother and all, and of course the blood reached me at once; there was the cleansing, the love of God in my heart, and the joy of the whole company. I love and honor that brother today.

Openness can cost. That is why the first step into openness is probably a big break. But it is worth it.

6

Exhortation

THERE remains one further stage in revival fellowship, and a most important one. We have so far seen: walking with Jesus step by step; two-way brokenness; cups running over or not running over; walking in the light, letting God show sin as sin; then confession and cleansing in the blood; and finally, as God gives opportunity, giving glory to God by testifying to His dealings with sin and to the power of the blood, bringing liberation to the one who testifies and joy and often conviction to the hearts of the hearers. The one remaining point is MUTUAL EXHORTATION.

The early church was first and foremost a fellowship. They "continued in the apostles' doctrine and fellowship." They broke bread from house to house. When they met in worship, it was the very opposite of our present church services, divided into the two categories of preacher and preached-to. It was a living fellowship in action. All took part, and there was such a flow of the Spirit through the believers that Paul had to write words of restraint. "How is it, brethren? When ye come together, *every one of you* hath a psalm, hath a doctrine. . . ."

Then he urged them to orderliness, and said that if while one was giving his word another arose with a desire to say something, let the first sit down and give place to him, for "the spirit of the prophets is subject to the prophets."

But today we have to *persuade* people to say something on those occasions when we have a time of open fellowship! Paul had to persuade them to keep silent and give the other fellow a chance! We have now replaced fellowshiping by preaching in our modern church life, and the reason is not hard to find. Fellowshiping necessitates a real flow of life in the fellowship, for each person has to be ready to contribute his share of what the Lord is really saying to him; preaching is an easy way out for a not-too-living fellowship. Appoint the preacher and let *him* find the messages; we can sit still and take or leave what we hear, as we please! Probably the best balance was found in early Methodism, where John Wesley laid down that besides the preaching and teaching meetings, there must be a weekly class-meeting which was on a strictly fellowship basis, and all who attended were required to tell of the Lord's personal dealings that week, whether concerning sins, or answers to prayer, or opportunities of witness.

But in the Scriptures it is also obvious that an important part of this fellowshiping was to be mutual exhortation, not just public exhortation by a preacher but each one exhorting the other. In Hebrews it distinctly says that the reason for such exhortation is to keep each other from becoming "hardened through the deceitfulness of sin" (3:13); in other words, lest our cups should cease to run over and we should not even recognize it. And it was to be daily exhortation! The same is said in 10:24–25, about public gatherings. The phrase usually quoted as a summons to attend weekly preaching services, "not forsaking the assembling of yourselves together," is actually used not of preaching but about mutual exhortation, and "so much the more, as ye see the day approaching." In James 5:16, also, we are exhorted to mutual confession of sin, especially that we may pray one for another.

In Africa I found these instructions being obeyed in all simplicity, and perhaps that one thing has contributed more than any other to the spread of revival. Those simple revived believers often use unusual boldness in question-

ing into the lives of those they contact, inquir-
ing as to what is their real spiritual condition
and experience of daily victory. Of course, such
boldness has also met with intense opposition,
and often also criticism, where the questioning
might not always have been wise, instead of
thankfulness that a few are bold when most of
the church is asleep! But it has certainly resulted
in a marvelous spread of revival and salvation
among saved and unsaved. It has had another
healthy effect also. It allows the Spirit to have
leadership, and not just some outstanding man.
Having accepted among themselves this healthy
principle of mutual exhortation, no man or leader
is put on some pedestal where he cannot be ap-
proached or questioned. All are brethren around
one Father, and if the very chiefest among those
brethren is seen by the spirit of discernment to
be unwise in leadership or to be off color spiritually, others will walk in the light with him.

In other words, the standard is that all want
to be the best for Jesus, all recognize how easily
deceived we are by Satan and the flesh, so all
desire their brethren to "exhort" them, if things
are seen in their walk which are not "the high-
est." Such exhortations are not easy either to
receive or give. To receive them with humility
and a readiness to be constantly adjusted before

God is one proof of continuing revival, for where we are not revived we almost certainly resent such challenges and reveal hurt self. To give them in grace and faithfulness costs perhaps even more. We are so easily tempted to "let well enough alone," or say, "It is not my business," and so forth, because we recognize that to bring such a challenge might disturb the peace or disrupt a friendship. But in revival we see we are our brother's keeper not for his sake but for Jesus' sake. When a brother is not on top spiritually, it wounds the Lord Jesus, it grieves Him, it hinders the working of His Spirit; therefore it is part of our duty to Him to be faithful to the brother. Not to be so is sin.

Of course, such challenging has to be deeply in the Spirit; that is to say, its source must be godly concern for the brother in question. We must always watch against the subtle danger of using such a method to "put a brother right," or even "to get our own back." Thus, it can only proceed from brokenness in ourselves. Indeed, often the only God-sealed approach may be not the pointing finger of accusation towards the brother but pointing back to ourselves, perhaps telling him of some reaction in ourselves caused by his conduct which we have had to take to the cross; or perhaps telling him how on some other occasion God had to deal with us through another brother's faithfulness. The golden rule, as it applies to challenging, is Matthew 7:12, "All things whatsoever ye would that men should do to you, do ye even so to them."

7

Revival

THIS completes what has been on my heart and mind to outline as God's way of continuous revival. I doubt that the use of much further actual illustration would add a great deal. However, I'll mention a few general points I have learned in fellowship with others who have formed the habit of regularly testifying one to the other of God's immediate dealings in their lives. Many of these testimonies tell, in simplest form, about the first seed of some sin (such as worldly ambition) getting into hearts, and how they have repented and been cleansed afresh in the blood. The thrill and value of such testimonies to me has been to see such sensitiveness to sin that when the seeds are first sown by Satan in the heart they are recognized in God's light and *dealt with*—whereas, in so many of us, we let such seeds lie and send down their roots until ultimately they bear their evil fruit openly.

I have seen in Africa immediate sensitiveness

to sin such as I had never seen it before. I had become used to hearing about or seeing the tragedy of a fine young life, apparently fully dedicated to Christ and serving Him, suddenly switched off to the service of the world through love of material gain, a much bigger salary, finer clothes, more possessions (all these things are now pouring into Africa)—but how well I knew that this did not happen in a moment. There were seeds of covetousness deep down in the heart, roots taking hold downwards and finally bearing their evil fruit upwards, but no one ever knew they were there! The walls were up and nothing was ever said about the inner struggle which finally ended in defeat. But when believers would tell about those inner struggles, what a thrill it was to hear one and another stand up to openly share about how "desires for progress" got hold of their hearts that week, and that they had seen that to love anything more than Jesus was *sin*. They had brought it to the cleansing blood and the sin was dealt with in its seed form!

The same picture applies to the awful hold on lives of the sins of uncleanness. So many times nothing is seen or known till the fall, be it fornication or adultery, has taken place and become public, and disciplinary action by the church becomes necessary. But where revival is and walls are down, the first motions of those sins in impure thoughts or unclean looks are recognized as *sin*, judged, confessed and brought to the cleansing blood—and it has never brought me embarrassment but rather joy to hear a brother testify to the Lord's dealings with him that week in his thought life.

Then there is the constant flow of *joy and praise* which results from such testimonies. It is the very opposite to some morbid, depressing accounts of sins committed. Each testimony magnifies the precious blood; indeed, I have never before seen the blood so praised and so precious, and hymns and choruses so much centering on "the fountain opened for uncleanness and sin," such as:

> *Glory, glory hallelujah,*
> *Glory, glory to the Lamb!*
> *Oh, the cleansing blood has reached me,*
> *Glory, glory to the Lamb!*

One other point I noticed was the *quickness* with which many have learned to "break" when conscious of sin. Whereas we so often remain unbroken and unrepentant for hours or days, too proud to break and witness—and thus we remain in darkness and heaviness of heart when we might come straight back into the light through the blood. In Africa again, in a formal Sunday morning service, I saw an interpreter who had been corrected in a mistaken interpretation by someone in the congregation stand up five minutes later, as the service ended, to tell the whole congregation that God had dealt with him for having resentment and pride in his heart because he had been corrected. Not only did he have an immediate restoration of the joy of the Lord, instead of carrying about hardness and resentment perhaps for days, but the testimony released a moving of the Spirit among the people, who carried on testimony and praise meetings in groups outside the building.

One final word about the way revival starts. It begins by one person seeing from God what it is to walk in the light. But to walk with Jesus like this involves also walking in the light with one another, relating horizontally as well as vertically, and that means there is at least one other person with whom to walk in open fellowship. Of course, as one brother said to me, "One would most naturally start walking like that with the person nearest to you—husband with wife, brother with sister, friend with friend." In other words, revival starts with *two* people being revived, and generally starts at home!

The way to begin walking in the light in fellowship one with another in a more public sense is to just *start*. I have found it most helpful, after talking with a congregation on the subject, to suggest that we move straight on to a time of quiet open fellowship. There will be no pressure, no demands made on any, but just an opportunity given to anyone to say anything, if they know the Spirit is telling them to do so. If others have no special word from God in their hearts, they are right to keep silent. But revival comes through *obedience*. Indeed, revival is really just obeying the Holy Spirit. Where He tells to "break" and to testify to the light shining on sin in our lives, and on the blood which cleanses from all sin, then let us obey, and we will find at once that the Spirit is loosed in revival in our own hearts and is moving in revival in the company.

I have found it good to make this time of open fellowship a natural *continuation* of a meeting, rather than to ask folks to go into another room. We are not aiming at an after-meeting in the ordinary sense when folks are called upon to make some crisis decision, but rather we want to practice a season of fellowship in which folks can see and learn and share in walking in the light, for we are not seeking for some sudden decisions but to learn the way of walking in revival individually and as communities.

Yet let us keep always before us that we are learning a *continuous* walk with God and one another. Any set practice can easily become formal and legalistic. A regularly scheduled "fellowship meeting" can become the "official" time for open fellowship, whereas we are seeking to learn to walk *all the time* in the two-way fellowship: in the home, between husband and wife and children; in our church and social contacts; and in our business life. It is by this means that the revival will spread among saved and unsaved . . . when God has thousands walking in revival who can't help witnessing to the ways in which God is meeting them in the dusty walks of their daily lives.

•   •   •

With these rough outlines I close this small book. The blessed Holy Spirit can never be systematized. The wind bloweth where it listeth. He is always original, and all our fresh springs are in Him. We can, however, at least give humble testimony to this His way which has been revealed to us in our day—even as Paul told the Corinthians that he was sending them Timothy to "bring you into remembrance of my ways which be in Christ." We write what we have seen and heard, and what we have tested by experience. May the Lord water the seed in hearts. God's plan in these last days is revival in His world-wide church, and through the revived church the reaping of a final great harvest of souls. I believe that what is outlined in these pages is the way of the Spirit, within the reach of all believers, both to begin and continue such a revival.

This book was produced by CLC Publications. We hope it has been life-changing and has given you a fresh experience of God through the work of the Holy Spirit. CLC Publications is an outreach of CLC Ministries International, a global literature mission with work in over 50 countries. If you would like to know more about us or are interested in opportunities to serve with a faith mission, we invite you to contact us at:

CLC Ministries International
P.O. Box 1449
Fort Washington, PA 19034

—

Phone: (215) 542-1242
E-mail: clcmail@clcusa.org
Websites: www.clcusa.org
www.clcpublications.com

READ THE REMARKABLE STORY OF

the founding of
CLC International

"Any who doubt that Elijah's God still lives ought to read of the money supplied when needed, the stores and houses provided and the appearance of personnel in answer to prayer.

—Moody Monthly

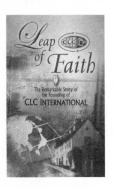

Is it possible that the printing press, the editor's desk, the Christian bookstore, and the mail order department, can glow with the fast-moving drama of an "Acts of the Apostles"?

Find out, as you are carried from two people in an upstairs bookroom to a worldwide chain of Christian bookcenters, multiplied by nothing but a "shoestring" of faith and committed, though sometimes unlikely, lives.

(Spanish edition)

CONTINUOUS REVIVAL

In this little book the author seeks to relate his experience and describe the effect on his life of the brokenness and ongoing personal revival which came as a result of his exposure to the teaching flowing from the Revival Movement in Ruanda, East Africa.

What he shares will change your life also if you are prepared to allow God to speak to you in the same way.

ISBN 958-8217-02-4

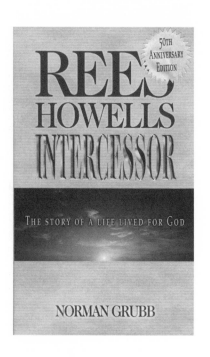

REES HOWELLS, INTERCESSOR

"A Welsh miner who became a spiritual giant. Here is the inspiring biography for all who seek to do exploits for God. It will inspire both young and old."—*Moody Monthly*

ISBN 0-87508-188-6

C.T. STUDD

In the history of missions, the career of C.T. Studd is exemplary. The author shows how the great sportsman renounced wealth and position to take up work for Christ.

ISBN 0-87508-202-5

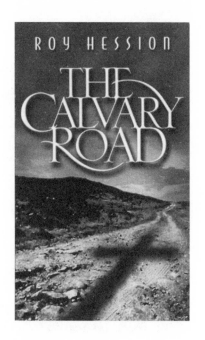

THE CALVARY ROAD

Many thousands have been richly blessed through the ministry of this book.

"This is one of the books that made the greatest impact on me as a young Christian, and in the work of *Operation Mobilization* around the world. We felt the message of this book was so important that it has been required reading for all who unite with us."

George Verwer, Operation Mobilization.

Trade Paper ISBN 0-87508-788-4
Mass Market ISBN 0-87508-236-X

WE WOULD SEE JESUS

We Would See Jesus is an amplification of Roy Hession's well-known *Calvary Road*.

In *We Would See Jesus* he ably points out that increased Bible knowledge and emphasis on service for God fall short of God's redemptive plan.

The direction and theme is — Jesus — "The Lord Jesus has come to release us from every yoke of bondage and to set us free to serve Him in the freshness and spontaneity of the Spirit."

To see Jesus is the answer to every aspect of our Christian life.

ISBN 0-87508-452-4